Joyful Creation Series

It's a Jungle in Here

Written and illustrated by
Kristie Wilde

Published by Wilde Art Press
10 9 8 7 6 5 4 3 2 1

It's a Jungle in Here

ISBN-13: 978-0-9974828-2-9
ISBN-10: 0-9974828-2-9

To my wonderful grandchildren,
and all children everywhere -
I love the way God created each one of you -
such wonderful variety!
He made you just the way you are because
that's how He wants you to be, for His glory and purpose.
You are beautifully created.
Thank you Jesus, for Your unsurpassed wisdom and grace ~

God loves variety, so . . .

He made lots of it in the jungle!

He made butterflies that stand out . . .

some that blend in, and some
that do both.

God made some cats **BIG** . . .

He made some frogs small . . .

very small!

God made **HUGE** elephants . . .

that can't hide very well.

And, He made small,
Stretchy-tongued
chameleons . . .

that can be hard to find!

God made some
VERY LOUD birds . . .

and very quiet Okapi.

He made monkeys of all sizes,
shapes and colors.

He was pleased.

Whether you stand out or blend in, are loud
or quiet, however you are . . .

God is especially happy
with how He made you!

"And God created great whales, and every living creature that moves, which the waters brought forth abundantly, after their kind, and every winged fowl after his kind: and God saw that it was good." Genisis 1:21, KJV

Tropical Butterflies: Emerald Swallowtail, Blue Morpho, and Leaf Wing Butterflies are created to blend in with their surroundings. The underside of their wings, which shows at rest with wings closed,

usually blends in with the earth, while the top blends in with what a hungry bird sees from above - trees and water. Some butterfly wings reflect the sunlight, flashing as they fly, confusing their predators.

Tigers, Leopards and Lions, can roar and run very fast. They're cousins to our house cats, but MUCH bigger. While they may look cute, they are to be respected.

Tropical Frogs: The Milk frog, Red Eyed tree frog and Imbabura tree frog live in humid parts of the jungle, in trees and bushes near slow moving water, like streams or ponds. These 2 to 4 inch frogs like to eat bugs.

Elephants are the worlds largest land animal. They have long trunks for smelling, breathing drinking and much more. They can rip branches off trees or pick up a blade of grass. Their tusks are part of their tooth structure. Elephants remember things for a long time.

"And God made the beast of the earth after his kind, and cattle after their kind, and everything that creeps upon the earth after his kind: and God saw that it was good." Genisis 1:25, KJV

Chameleons: There are many species of Chameleons ranging in size from ½ inch to 27 inches. Their eyes move separately so they can see all the way around. A chameleon's skin changes color to blend in with their surroundings or mood. Bugs are their favorie snack food!

Tropical Birds: Tucans, and Macaws can be VERY loud. These birds are brightly colored to blend in with the colors high up in the trees where they live. Flamingos, who are also very loud, like to hang out in shallow muddy areas, where they make their nests out of mud. Their feather color comes from the shrimp they eat.

Okapi are at home in the lush rain forests of a small part of Central Africa, and are most closely related to the giraffe. They communicate with sounds that are so low pitched we can't hear them - but they can hear each other! An Okapi's tongue is long enough that they can clean their eyes with it!

Monkeys like the Macaques, Mantled Guereza and Proboscis, live in trees. They use their tails to help them swing and travel from tree to tree. Some monkeys like to swim while others don't.

For You formed my inward parts; You wove me in my mother's womb. Psalms 139: 13

"And God saw everything that he had made, and, behold, it was very good."Genisis 1:31

Author and Illustrator, Kristie Wilde

As a mother and Grandmother, Kristie Wilde enjoys going on adventures with children. She loves to see their eyes light up as they discover some new, exciting treasure – especially when that treasure is a bit of insight about God and His creation. She endeavors to establish a solid, God affirming foundation in their lives.

Kristie has a degree in Forestry and blends her knowledge of the natural world with her artistic gift and her love for Jesus to create beautiful, insightful children's books that light up the eyes of their readers.

She is the author, illustrator and publisher for the *Joyful Creation Series*: *Made For a Purpose*, *So Great a Love*, and this book, *It's a Jungle in Here*.

Kristie has also illustrated and published Judy Watson's delightful children's books, *Shooting Stars and Satellites*, *Green Smoothies and Brain Talk*, *All About Me*, and *In My World*.

The US Forest Service and Tri Dam have commissioned her to illustrate interpretive signage for them along the Highway 108 corridor through the Sierras.

As the owner and artistic source of *Wilde Art*, and *Wilde Art Press* in Sonora, California, she enlivens her projects with watercolor illustrations in a realistic style with whimsical touches.
Combining her talent as an artist and illustrator, her expertise in Photoshop and her experience communicating educational concepts - gained while working with the Interpretive Department of the U.S. Forest Service - she manages projects from concept to completion.

More works by Kristie can be seen on her websites: wilde-art.com and wildeartpress.com, and she can be contacted by email at kristie@wilde-art.com.

CPSIA information can be obtained
at www.ICGtesting.com
Printed in the USA
BVHW02n0925160518
516407BV00002B/10/P

9 780997 482829